The Nature Kid's Guide to
MEERKATS

RENATA MARIE

LP Media Inc. Publishing
Text copyright © 2023 by LP Media Inc.
All rights reserved.

No part of this book may be reproduced or transmitted in any form or by any means,
electronic or mechanical, including photocopying, recording, or by an information storage
and retrieval system — except by a reviewer who may quote brief passages in a review to be
printed in a magazine or newspaper — without permission in writing from the publisher.

For information address LP Media Inc. Publishing,
3178 253rd Ave. NW, Isanti, MN 55040
www.lpmedia.org

Publication Data

Meerkats
The Nature Kid's Guide to Meerkats — First edition.

Summary: "Learn all about Meerkats, the Nature Kid Way"
— Provided by publisher.

ISBN: 978-1-954288-67-6

[1. Meerkats – Non-Fiction] I. Title.

Title: The Nature Kid's Guide to Meerkats

CONTENTS

Stand Tall 4

Sand Everywhere 6

Underground Home 8

Digging for Dinner 10

Biting Bugs 12

Keep Watch 14

Bolt Holes 16

Be Scary 18

Fight and Bite 20

Sunbathing 22

Peeping Pups 24

Pup-Sitters 26

Big Boss 28

Kat Land 30

Many Dangers 32

Rainy Days 34

War Dance 36

Strong Together 38

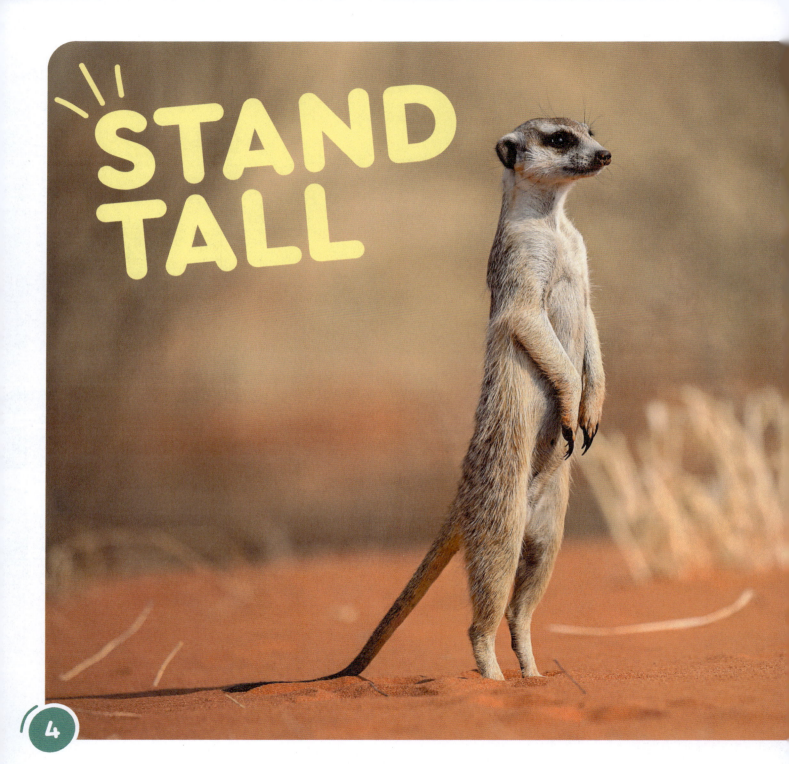

Peep! **A meerkat stands tall. He watches the dry land.**

Meerkats live in Africa. The sun is hot. The sky is clear. The ground is sandy. The grass grows tall. And predators are everywhere.

But meerkats are strong fighters. They do what they must to keep their families safe.

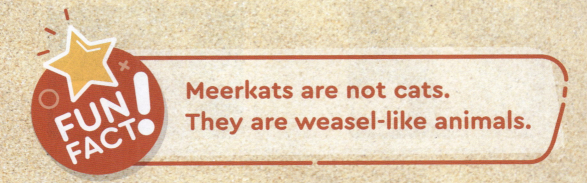

FUN FACT! Meerkats are not cats. They are weasel-like animals.

SAND EVERYWHERE

FUN FACT!

Meerkat claws are 0.8 inches (2 cm) long.

Sand flies everywhere. A meerkat digs.

Meerkats have long, sharp claws. Each paw has four toes. They shovel sand away from the hole. Their long bodies reach deep into the ground. Each eye has a clear eyelid. It keeps their eyes safe from the sand. Their ears close to keep out dirt.

Meerkats are the perfect size for digging tunnels. They are up to 14 inches (36 centimeters) long. They weigh up to two pounds (0.9 kilograms). Females are a bit bigger than males.

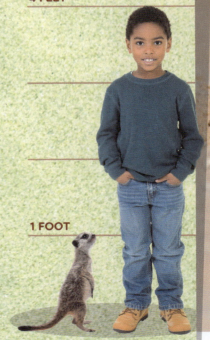

UNDER-GROUND HOME

A meerkat dives into a tunnel. It is dark and safe.

Meerkats dig a lot of tunnels. The tunnels can be 16 feet (4.9 meters) long. They have up to 15 ways to get in and out. They have two to three levels. Some are 6.5 feet (2 m) deep. They have rooms. One is for sleeping. One is for baby meerkats. One is even for going to the bathroom.

Meerkats are safe in their tunnels. They hide from predators. They stay out of the rain.

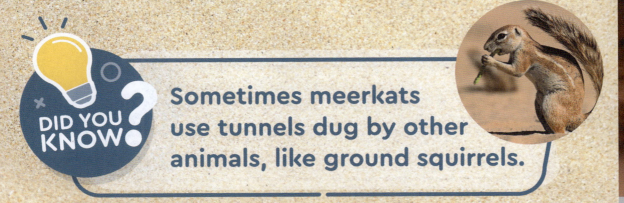

DID YOU KNOW? Sometimes meerkats use tunnels dug by other animals, like ground squirrels.

DIGGING FOR DINNER

Sniff ... Scratch ... A meerkat digs for dinner.

Meerkats have strong noses. They smell the ground. **They can even smell their prey through the sand.**

When they find prey, they dig—fast. They stick their pointy noses into the hole. They can fit it into tiny spaces where animals hide. Then they catch their food. Their teeth are sharp.

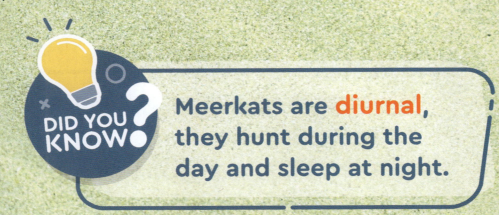

DID YOU KNOW? Meerkats are diurnal, they hunt during the day and sleep at night.

BITING BUGS

Beetle Eggs Scorpion Snail Spider

Crunch! **A meerkat bites a bug.**

Meerkats are omnivores. **They eat meat and plants.** They eat beetles and caterpillars. They eat birds and eggs. They eat fruit, snails, and mice. They even eat spiders and scorpions.

If a meerkat is stung by a scorpion, it will not be hurt. They are immune.

FUN FACT! Meerkats work together when they face big prey like lizards.

KEEP WATCH

DID YOU KNOW?

Meerkats have dark spots around their eyes. They keep the sun out, just like the black marks under football players' eyes.

**Sun shines on a meerkat.
He stands tall on a rock.**

Meerkats have their heads in the ground a lot. And predators are everywhere. **While other meerkats hunt, one keeps watch.**

A meerkat climbs a rock or bush. It stands on its back legs. It uses its tail like a third leg. It holds its head high.

Meerkats have sharp eyes. They peep to tell their families they are safe. If they see danger, they bark or whistle. And it is a race to the tunnels.

BOLT HOLES

Jackal

Eagle

Snake

An eagle swoops over the meerkats. A meerkat barks.

Meerkats have to watch out for falcons and hawks. They watch out for eagles, snakes, and jackals.

If they hear a warning bark, they run to bolt-holes. The bolt holes are big. More than one meerkat can fit at a time, so more can get to safety quicker.

Meerkats can remember where thousands of bolt holes are.

DID YOU KNOW?

Meerkats use different calls for predators. They have one call for predators on land and one for predators in the air.

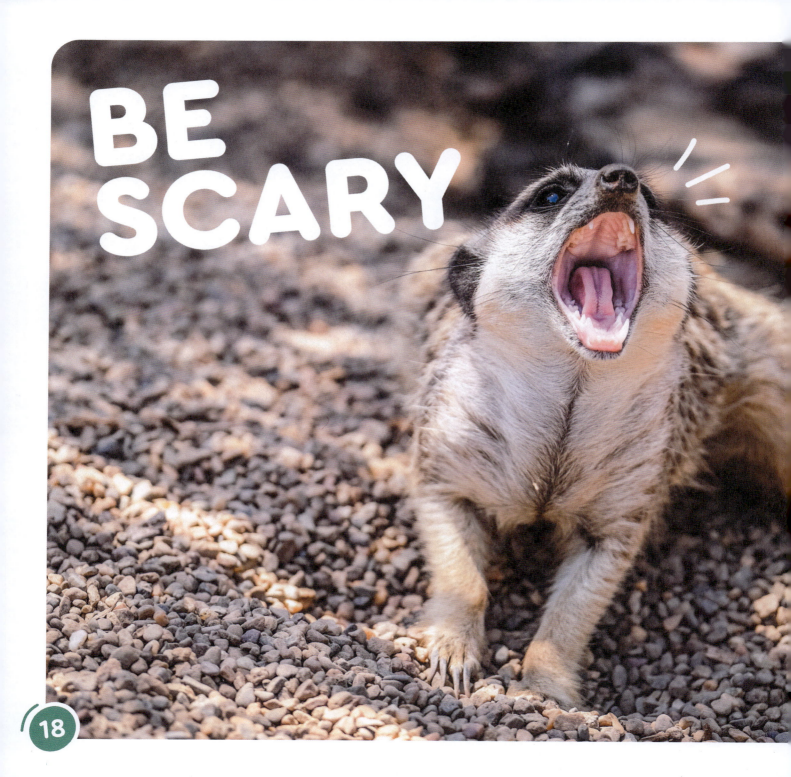

A meerkat runs, but the bolt-hole is far. And the eagle is close.

Sometimes, meerkats get stuck in the open. When they do, they try to look scary. They lie on their backs. They stick their sharp claws in the air. They show their teeth.

If meerkats are in a group, they hiss. They puff up their fur. They try to look big together. They hope the predator will think they are one big animal.

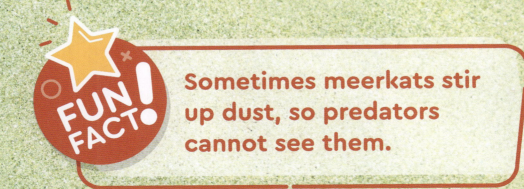

FUN FACT! Sometimes meerkats stir up dust, so predators cannot see them.

FIGHT AND BITE

A snake eyes a young meerkat. But the meerkat calls for his family.

Snakes are dangerous. They want to eat meerkats. **But meerkats fight back.**

Together, they circle the snake. The snake strikes. But the meerkats stay far enough away. The meerkats try to look big. They bite and claw. Soon, the snake gets tired. It leaves as fast as it can. The meerkats' land is safe again.

FUN FACT! Meerkats are immune to some snake bites.

Meerkats lie in the sun. They are safe and warm.

When the sun rises, meerkats come out of the tunnels. They stand up on their back legs. **They warm their bellies in the sun.** They lie in the sand together. They lick each other's fur. When the sun is too hot, they lie on rocks to stay cool.

DID YOU KNOW? Meerkats groom each other to keep their families close.

PEEPING PUPS

24

Peep! **A little meerkat peeks out of a hole. She is closely followed by her siblings.**

Baby meerkats are called pups. They are born mostly hairless and with their eyes and ears closed. They live in the tunnels, where it is safe.

Their eyes open in two weeks. At three weeks, they eat more than milk. And at four weeks, they take their first steps out of the tunnels.

FUN FACT! Meerkat pups only weigh up to 1.3 ounces (37 grams) when they are born.

PUP-SITTERS

FUN FACT! Meerkats purr when they are happy.

The mother leaves to hunt. She needs food to make more milk. But another meerkat watches the pups.

Meerkats work together to raise the pups. There are usually three to four pups in a group. They do not know how to stay safe. The pup-sitters teach them how to hide, clean, and fight. They teach them what is safe to eat.

Mother meerkats bring back live scorpions. They bite off the stingers. The pups have to learn how to safely hunt them.

The mother returns.
She is in charge.

Meerkats live in groups called **mobs**. They have up to 40 meerkats.

One meerkat leads them all. **The leader is a female.** She births most of the pups. She does not want other females to have pups.

She will get rid of pups that are not hers. She will kick out females that have pups. She wants her pups to have enough care and food.

DID YOU KNOW? Female meerkats without pups still make milk. That way, they can feed the lead female's pups.

A group of meerkats walks around their land. It is theirs. And they will keep it safe.

Meerkats have more than one set of tunnels. The tunnels are all throughout their land. Sometimes they move to a new tunnel.

They walk around their land and leave a mark. They rub their smell on rocks and plants. Other meerkat mobs live nearby. They want them to stay away. But sometimes, lands overlap. And the fights can be scary.

FUN FACT! A meerkat mob's land can be four square miles (10 square kilometers).

MANY DANGERS

DID YOU KNOW? There are around 500,000 meerkats in the wild.

A meerkat races to the tunnels. Danger is near.

There are many meerkats. **They are not in danger of dying out.** But they still face dangers. They watch out for predators. They watch out for bad weather. They watch out for humans. They even have to watch out for other meerkats.

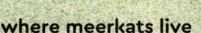
where meerkats live

RAINY DAYS

34

Rain washes over the sand. It pools. It grows. And it flows into tunnels.

As the Earth warms, there are more floods. Water fills the meerkat's tunnels. They have to leave them to live. There are also more droughts. When the land is dry, there is less food. And meerkats have to fight to eat.

KIDS CAN HELP THE EARTH

Turn the lights off

Throw away less food

Take shorter showers

Tails are high. Backs are rounded. This is war.

Meerkats do not like other mobs on their land. **When they see other meerkats, they do a war dance.** They stick their tails up. They round their backs. They kick their feet. If they can look big, the other meerkats might leave. If not, they will charge.

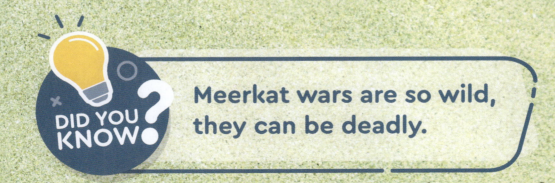

DID YOU KNOW? Meerkat wars are so wild, they can be deadly.

The ground shakes. It booms. The meerkats are scared.

Humans also hurt meerkats. They build large roads. The roads are hard to cross for small animals.

They trap meerkats for pets. But meerkats do not do well as pets. They need their families.

Families keep meerkats safe. Together, they can face any danger.

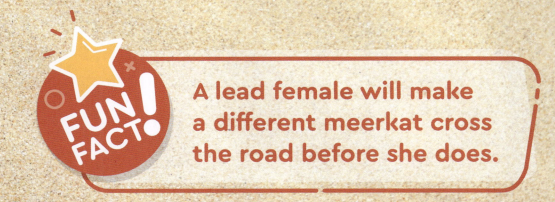

FUN FACT!

A lead female will make a different meerkat cross the road before she does.

GLOSSARY

diurnal
an animal is active during the day and rests at night
page 11

bolt-hole
a safe hole dug by meerkats near their hunting areas to use when there is danger
page 17

immune
kept safe from something that can hurt
page 13

omnivores
animals that eat meat and plants
page 13

mob
a group of 10–40 meerkats all living together as one pack
page 29

war dance
a dance that scares away other meerkat mobs
page 37

MORE AMAZING ANIMAL BOOKS
from Nature Kids Publishing!

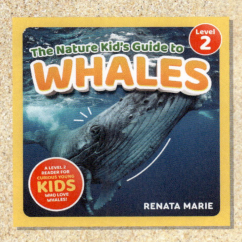 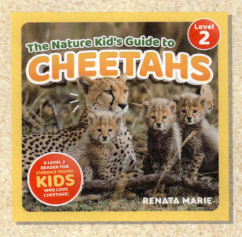

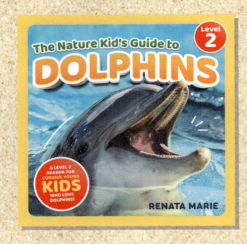 

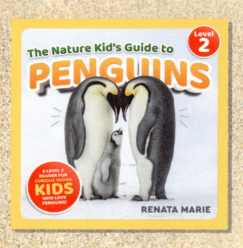
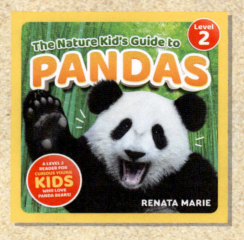

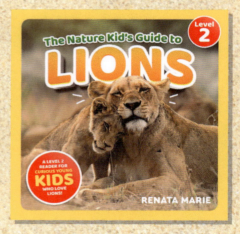

Visit NatureKidsPublishing.com
to Learn More!

Printed in Great Britain
by Amazon